Man is in love and loves what vanishes,
what more is there to say?

~ W. B. Yeats,
"Nineteen Hundred and Nineteen"

Also by Christopher Levenson

In Transit, part of the three-volume, New Poets 1959 (edited by Edwin Muir, Eyre & Spottiswood, London, 1959)

Cairns, Chatto & Windus, London, UK 1969

Stills, Chatto & Windus, London, UK 1972

Into the open, Golden Dog Press, Ottawa, ON 1977

The Journey Back, Sesame Press, Windsor, ON. 1978

Arriving at night, Mosaic Press, Oakville, ON. 1986

Half Truths, Wolsak & Wynn, Toronto, ON 1990

Duplicities (new and selected poems)
Mosaic Press, Oakville. ON,1993

The Bridge, Buschek Books, Ottawa, ON 2000

Local Time, Stone Flower Press, Ottawa, ON 2006

Night Vision, Quattro Books, Toronto, ON 2014

A tattered coat upon a stick. Quattro Books, Toronto, ON 2017

Small Talk

by

Christopher Levenson

720 – Sixth Street, Box # 5
New Westminster, BC
CANADA V3C 3C5

Title: Small Talk
Author: Christopher Levenson
Cover Photo:"Chit Chat" courtesy of Barrie Jones
      Collective Agency Project
      City of Vancouver public art program.
Author Photo: Oonagh Berry (back cover)
Layout/Edit/Design: Candice James

www.silverbowpublishing.com
© Silver Bow Publishing
info@silverbowpublishing.com

isbn: 9781774032152 book
isbn: 9781774032169 e-book

Library and Archives Canada Cataloguing in Publication

Title: Small talk / by Christopher Levenson.
Names: Levenson, Christopher, 1934- author.
Description: Includes index.
Identifiers: Canadiana (print) 20220220751 | Canadiana (ebook) 2022022076X | ISBN 9781774032152
  (softcover) | ISBN 9781774032169 (HTML)
Classification: LCC PS8573.E945 S63 2022 | DDC C811/.54—dc23

For Oonagh

Acknowledgements

First of all, many thanks to Kieran Egan, Tom Gorman and Ken Klonsky as well, as always, to Oonagh Berry, my wife, all of whom have read through and helped me select and organize these poems. A few of them are taken from my earlier books, while others have appeared in *Grain*, *Painted Bride Quarterly. Pocket Lint* and the on-line *Your daily poem.*

Foreword

Why short poems? Although compactness and density are important poetic virtues, I never set out to write poems of a certain length: a poem should be as long as it needs to be and not a syllable longer. But small things risk going unnoticed. Thus, although some of these poems have appeared in my previous twelve books, since most reviewers focus on the supposedly more 'serious' longer poems, they have received little attention.

Moreover, because many Canadian poets still seem self-consciously caught up in creating the 'great Canadian poem', the national literary monument, those qualities of irony and wit, as distinct from broad humour and whimsy, that often characterize short poems tend not to be so highly prized. For the most part, Canadian poets – P.K. Page and Pat Lowther are two BC exceptions – are more likely to honour Whitman than Dickinson.

Obviously short poems are best suited for epigrammatic insights into public life, the verbal equivalent of a good political cartoon, as also for thumbnail sketches of people, animals or cityscapes. Just as in painting, sometimes, an oil sketch or an apparently slight drawing will elicit an atmosphere, a charm and a sense of transience denied to the more solemn, fully finished masterpiece – think Rembrandt, Watteau, Goya, Daumier – so too, I hope, some of these snapshots will capture, in passing, aspects of everyday life that we otherwise might have forgotten to see.

The way I have divided up the book is arbitrary, basically by subject matter rather than by theme, but unlike a regular book of poetry where one eventually reads the whole work, these poems invite random dipping. If some of them give the reader momentary pause, I shall be satisfied.*~ Christopher Levenson*

Contents

Beasts

Landscapes

Garlands

Of the World

Beasts

Lion

Heraldry got it all wrong; they are not
rampant and noble. Most of the time
they are just layabouts, sunning on rocks, complacent
and chauvinist. But it shows
what a good coiffure and a deep voice can do
for your self-esteem, that plus a bit of land
to spray and call your own and defend as long as you can
till someone with a louder voice, younger body, stronger teeth
drives you away into the veldt, alone.

Lemur

A star of the silver screen,
shyly wrapped in her furs,
she wants to be left alone
with her luminous eyes in the dark.

Camel

Kalu, *'the dark one'*: for three hours near Jaiselmer
I lurched headlong on your back, your bridle jingling
at the edge of the Thar desert. I was relieved to find you,
though harumphing, not supercilious,
just a placid rental beast. Since then, I carry round
an ingrowing hump of memory
to draw upon in dry times.

Aardvark

Prize slob of the animal kingdom, slum dweller.
The two I saw in Philadelphia Zoo,
sprawled like dead drunks on their concrete floor,
were snoring like humans. All that was missing:
beer cans and a TV remote.

Giraffe

Dream-like acrobats, above it all but not
aloof, gainly, living geometry,
moving in unison, legs and necks
against a slow-motion backdrop
of golden veldt grass
to curl their long tongues around
succulent foliage.
Sleepwalkers, their camouflage
is useless but beautiful.

Giant Sloth

Easy does it, I say,
one step at a time.
In any case to me
the world makes more sense
upside down.
I believe in taking my time,
mostly my night time.
Live and let live, that's my
philosophy.

Armadillo

Relax, mini dinosaur:
I have no designs
on your armour. For me
you're not a basket case.
Unroll, I'll let you be,
recluse.

Squirrel

High-wire Baryshnikov,
you pirouette between trees,
dancing on air, creating
in our backyard
new alphabets of space,
all flourish and curlicue,
calligraphies of fur.

Prairie Dogs

Once in Wyoming I saw some,
their rural slum paradigm
of mankind's teeming millions.
Each upstart head like a tent peg, cocky, abrasive.
In their own holes burrowing
or raising grubby empires
of earth, like us, mangy optimists
enjoying the transient sun.

Canada Geese

They cross the highway
in stately single file
with an air of entitlement.
Though hardly endangered,
are they somehow aware
that like loons and snowy owls
they have acquired heraldic status?
Despite themselves, everywhere
people stop to admire them.

Skunk

Forty years it took me
to acclimatize to that stink.
Now I would miss it
almost as much as the loon's cry.
Its signature penetrates
these woods, this countryside,
tells me I am at home.

Pigeons

Dapper, urbane,
aldermen of the bird world.
They observe a bureaucratic
pecking order, discreetly
inspect the crumbs they are thrown.
Later they whitewash the statues
of discredited soldiers and statesmen.

Leech

This isn't going to hurt one little bit. As I bite
I anaesthetize, draw blood,
to let evil spirits out, to salvage
severed appendages. The flow
continues. Antiseptic
secretes from my body, protective
pharmacy. I'm so attached to you,
dear patient, I do you good.
My tongue scoops out everything alien,
restores, leaving you clean.

Surprise

A perfect specimen, he thought,
the wildlife biologist, stuffing
a snowy owl into the lab freezer
overnight for safe keeping, along
with some smaller rodents and fish.
When he returned next day
the owl stared at him, wide-eyed,
having feasted long and well
on the more authentic dead.

Visiting the river otters

Ripples betrayed them even before their wet backs
clambered onto the ledge, the distinctive tail
neither muskrat nor beaver. We stayed an hour,
gazing down from the Minto bridges, enthralled
by sinuous play, headlong plunges, slapstick battles,
while their slick inquisitive faces
looked back at us, acrobats seeking applause.

Salamander

An adman's dream, its psychedelic colours
make it a friendly amphibian, alert but not slithery,
garishly halfway between frog and lizard
yet with a pedigree of legend, consumed
with chaste fire, undying courage.
No more today than a fashion statement,
it stands out against any background –
fall leaves, forest pools –
always obligingly svelte.

Hummingbird

Deftest of epicures,
this mini-tornado
sips with extended beak
from a snifter of hibiscus,
samples, moves on.

Koala

Cuddly layabout,
it too becomes addicted
to the human touch.

Wombat

Like a tightly packed weekend bag,
furry left luggage,
he dozes in hollow tree trunks,
waiting for nightfall.

Duck-billed Platypus

Not bad as a first draft, a committee
compromise, it sleeks back and forth underwater
in its own enclosure at the Melbourne Zoo,
a furry toy submarine.

Indoor cat

Fat white cat stretched out on the window ledge
of the ground floor flat opposite, do your eyes dilate
when you see chickadees hop on the lawn outside?
Do your claws itch? You seem to sit there at ease
or bored, content to acquiesce
in an imposed neutrality that lets
your hunting skills lie fallow. Only from close by
can I see that even in sleep your whiskers twitch.

My master

My master's a man of few words –
'Sit!', 'Heel!', 'Fetch!', 'Stay!' and sometimes 'Good Boy!'
My commander-in-chief carries a big stick.
What more could I want? Great Anubis, he smells delicious,
a mixture of sweat and tobacco and dirty socks.
At times when I lick his face or nuzzle his crotch
he scratches me under the chin, and it seems we are mates.
But I know my place and I'd happily die for him
if the occasion arose. I only regret
that he misses so much of the finer things in life,
week-old hamburger buns or a nice fresh turd.

Heron

Upright, he looks collapsible, some kind of
trick photographic contraption
as he picks his way, stilted, fastidious
down the early morning shoreline.
But let him fly, let him take off over water
with that huge steady wingbeat and his unmistakable
blue-grey shape is supreme.
Beak and head held back, legs trailing, he looks askance at
the chit-chat and squabbles of lesser birds, intent on
his own measured purposes.

Starlings

What a rowdy bunch! Like kids
in an inner-city playground,
squawking, scuffling in the dust,
their gang swoops in, takes over from
dapper slate-coloured juncos and chickadees,
and ruins the neighbourhood.

Panic

A flute bewilders us
through lucent evergreens
deeper into the shade,
its melody echoing
elusive bird calls ,
hints of a hidden stream.
till we come to,
come to ourselves.

Call waiting

From the further shore it emerges through the mist
and I want to say to the loon:
"Your call is important to us."

Landscapes

Small Flowers

You need to walk past slowly even to notice them
embossing crevices between the stones
of the sea wall only a metre above
the high water mark.
These tiny anonymous mauve flowers,
clustering in their thousands cushioned by moss,
somehow find room to thrive precariously.

Driftwood

Driftwood, nature's toy,
marbled by sunlight, water,
slowly becomes art.

Willows

Even the swallows' return is not more welcome
than the yellow green strands of the willow
in the yard next door, its long blond hair brushed out
after rinsing, glistening fresh.
The last trees to shed in the Fall and the Spring's first arrival,
they shake off the frost, crowd out the final snow.

Cornflowers

For all their astringent blue
assertiveness, cornflowers,
once cut from their native meadows,
last only days,
Courageously erect,
captive in a glass jar,
then wilting, they fade to white.

Grass

After the summer's drought persistent rain
spurs the parched roots. But even under
the boots of the conqueror, grass reasserts itself,
will not lie down and be still. Let's hear it for grass.

Log Cabin Point

The sun arrives late on green water, a rowboat
is moored to a makeshift dock, its planks now drying
after a day of rain. With the grass freshly varnished
with light and the willows' flickering stilled
over the reeds and lily pads, patiently evening shades
indulge our moods, meld liquid silences.

Turning point

Slowly the bones of the neighbourhood show through
vanishing leafwork. Concealed all summer long,
high-rises emerge from hiding. With the avenue shorn
of all its green distractions, clean lines once more
frame the bulk of bank and warehouse
and from the debris of bare stalk and branch
painstakingly create
greyprints for winter.

November

Another dawn without mountains.
From our fifth-floor balcony
slowly only local trees emerge.
After yesterday's blizzard of leaf
birds have their cover blown.
Across the road a soccer field loud with school kids.
Everything else clouded, leaden.

Balcony

In November red chinese lanterns
fill a yellow watering can
abandoned to the rain.

Lamps

Behind the backyard fence a lantern
broadcasts long spokes of light
over fresh snow. No matter
how far away, lamps humanize
nocturnal silence.

Winter sunrise

Sandbar clouds, streaks of mackerel sky
invoke this virulent sunrise
on the day of your funeral.

Garlands

The spiritualist

Voices molest her everywhere
as she flits blindly like a bat.
A wind-crazed bush of silver hair
burns like a halo through her hat.

Locked in her afterlife she cannot see
mere mortal visitors but stands
in her black habit of soliloquy
talking quietly to her distant friends.

Indian summer

Blown hair veils your face
but our children seem happy swimming
where yellow leaves ruffle the water.

Equilibrium
for Kate and Tom

Arriving unannounced, among shaded, small-town avenues,
white, clapboard houses overhung by elms,
I watch as they prepare breakfast. Kate
has now remarried, well.
They are clearly happy together.
Her new husband, Tom, a scientist,
has just published a book, *Equilibrium,*
a chemistry of solutions.

Garlands

Human honours in India are worn lightly.
Garlands of marigold or sandalwood
are no sooner given than doffed.
Only the dead get to keep theirs
as they flower into ash.

Grooming
for Nadine and Nadia

Nadine, for a moment only, at bedtime
combing her daughter's long hair,
teasing the skeins out, can feel
the other's gaze taken up in herself and answered
as she stands there, that younger self,
wide eyes still so full of hope,
nothing too tangled yet.

Ecology

Unlike oil, natural gas or the Amazon forest,
love is a renewable resource:
drill deep enough and you'll find it still welling up
from the bed of the ocean or flaring across Prairie
landscapes,
sweet, light, crude, whatever.

Techno-lovers

Even up at the cottage they cannot keep their hands off
each other's Blackberrys, I-Phones.
Down at the dock they are constantly fingering, checking
the markets, the playoffs, the office,
afraid they might, God forbid, for even a second
find themselves off the grid and feel compelled
to gaze at boring water, monotonous trees
or hear the tweeting of birds, be aware of the loon.

Old age

Old age is contagious.
Stick around long enough
and you'll be infected too.

The good shepherdess

In St Bavo Church, Haarlem,
a mildly overweight elderly lady from Kansas
exclaimed of a carving "My, that's really pretty!"
Her elderly husband nodded, made a snide inaudible joke.
He had spent his working life in board rooms,
departure lounges, at the Country Club.
Churches were not his thing, let alone works of art.
She understood, let it pass. Just as she did with her first born,
she swaddles him with attention, doesn't let him stray far.

Stroke

Buried alive in a stroke. At once
relatives, rescuers gather and with bare hands
heave to remove the boulders
at the mouth of his cave of silence.
A prisoner, a lifer, he must invent codes
to tap out what cannot be said.
All night they work by arc lamps to create,
while air remains, at least a tiny eyehole
to reduce the darkness, to stir
that first faint word again.

Manuscript

Seven decades illuminate
her parchment face
with unfinished history.

Vanity

Shifting my bathroom mirror I see myself
becoming a bureaucrat's dream,
submitted in triplicate.

At the cinema, Good Friday

Brisbane in early Fall
(though nothing falls here:
jacaranda, eucalyptus,
everything's evergreen)
I have come in from the mall,
anonymous in my invisible
slouch hat and mackintosh
to sit by myself in the plush dark.
It is Good Friday. I wait
for the show to begin.

At the party

Like icebergs we stand around,
brilliant but mostly submerged.
No one approaches.

Polyglot

Trust me, I can say nothing
in six different languages:
nichts, nada, niente, niets, ništa, rien.

Chameleon

Twice in the centre of Amsterdam strangers
have stopped me to ask for directions.
Maybe after more than fifty years
I am finally blending in here and my cane
makes me look like a heritage site
or a building that must be torn down
for the sake of the usual progress.
Translated: I am more than content
to pass for one of the locals.

Poet as cook

Others may measure their meat by cut or weight,
insist on tenderloin, shoulder. I specialize in
nuances of heart and tongue, their delicate flavours
marinaded in wine overnight and highly seasoned.
If my liver is not great and my fried brain
is only passable, just taste my sweetbreads,
judge me by my own lights.

Nutrition
for David Dorken

After victory Aztec warriors would
devour the hearts of brave slain enemies
to partake of their courage. So I like a cannibal
in a secondhand bookstore grab at my late colleague's
relics, trepan the skulls, bend back the spines, scoop up
a dozen books, hope to acquire some part of the brain,
a hint of the intellect they went to feed.

Transients

Great portraits are always contemporary.
I saw Helene Fourment today on the 24 bus
and Romney's Clergyman's daughter offered me tea
at the summer fete. In the local supermarket,
peasant heads by Breughel and Bosch inspected the lettuce.
Epstein's Jewess looked out from a doorway in Camden Town.
The eternal transfigured in the particular,
a hole in the fence around a building site.

Fall
for Carol and Don

The two of them sitting there
on lawn chairs a few feet apart,
scanning the Sunday papers
in a litter of unraked leaves,
are content to have this time alone
together in the garden's crisp shadows,
embraced by conifers, knowing
this may be the last time
she will savour the autumn.

Catch of the day

Memories, netted like fish
quivering with light, thrash daggers
in the dark hold of the brain.
No point in having more paintings than you have walls
to hang them on.

Profile

As you sketch me, draw me out,
out of my early morning comfort zone,
I am forced to regard myself
as proportion, shading, mass,
brief amalgam of ears, nose, bearded chin,
merely the first rough draft
of a human being.

Weeds

I am no good at gardening. I have black thumbs.
The Rhododendrons stiffen when I come near,
The rockery grows obdurately barren.
The sunflowers hang their heads.
.
Weeds make me most at home
and plants like vetch, wild rose, forget-me-nots
that take me as I am and thrive on neglect.
Untidy flourishers, resilient in the dirt,
adorning chaos at the highway's edge,–
these suit my mood.

For Virginia

Stoned with guilt, not for herself but for all
she had been made a part of, complicit
in the world's madness, she wades,
weighed down, into the black waters
and in the midst of war made her own peace.

Newsreel

In the newsclip from Liberia
the naked running boy,
when shot, did not get up
but lay in the dust quite still.
This was no stunt.
In the film of his life
he was not simply an extra,
he played the title role.

While you were out

God telephoned,
called to see you,
wants to see you,
will call again.
Please call him, collect.
He's always listening.

Pandemic

Things are so bad now
Charon refuses my coin,
insists on plastic.

Dead letter

The letter was marked *'Please forward'*
but the man it was meant for, a miner,
had already gone down in his cage.
Persephone, are you busy?
Next time you're down there, would you
do me a favour, deliver
this?

Of the World

Skyscraper

The skyscraper office block's sheer
effrontery
has one redeeming virtue:
its glossy sides reflect
oaks in the nearby park,
cloud transients, a veering gull -
contact prints of details that otherwise
I would have forgotten to see.

Noon

Stiletto sunlight
thrusts into alleyways.
A fugitive shadow lurks
under stairwells or behind
locked doors, will not
surrender, knows
its time will come again.

Yaletown

Highrise glaciers stacked
cascade in slow motion
into False Creek below.

Containers

Stacked in Halifax harbour
like toddlers' building blocks
abandoned at bedtime. No telling
what lurks inside, or who.

Weekend

Vacuity at noon, the light
irresolute, shifty behind
warehouses locked for the weekend.
'Vacancies' says the notice. Only
this creosote wooden fence guards
the unswept schoolyards drained of laughter.

Office

The sunset only stays
while the light is off
and the typewriters silent.
The woods are stained with russet,
the river is bleeding.
But when the lights are on
you can only see the darkness.

Legacy

West of Kitsilano streets named for trees -
arbutus, fir, laburnum, walnut, yew -
give way to battlefields, Waterloo, Blenheim, Trafalgar,
school history detritus.
Elsewhere lumber barons' family names
succumb to oblivion except for this
brief civic acknowledgment.
Believers in posterity would do better
to have their latinized names forever attached
to some newly discovered asteroid, insect, disease.

The silent majority

Wherever they are their voices,
lacking volume control, take over
and make us accomplices several tables away.
We eavesdrop on the cost of their last trip to Maui,
their views on Cuba, socialized medicine. It is as if
the whole world waits at every street corner to greet them
and cheer them on, to make them feel at home.
What's not to like? We practise acts of submission.

Mexico City

In the Zona Rosa the dark tinted glass
of the latest office high-rise reflects back upon
crowded pavements. Beside the airport freeway
monstrous billboards compete
with the blue of jacarandas
that floats over the neighbourhood
corner stores, auto workshops
like a pale dream of wealth and liberty.

One fine day

'Nagasaki – the sea, the harbour':
How could Puccini have known
that the Pinkerton man, dressed in black,
would return to secure his treasure?

Even with her telescope, Butterfly
could not foresee how decades later
her Little Boy would come home
with that ultimate American gift of light.

Dental hygienists

Dental hygienists,
the world's last moralists, *know*
what is best for you.

Quebec diner

As native speakers can we afford
to condescend when in a menu we find
our tongue so twisted
"French Fried Salad Greavy
Chief Salad, Day Soup" (They sound
like exotic frontier characters)
when we who were born as Anglos
with a greasy silver spoon in our mouths
are fluent neither in French nor cookery?

Spiders

Like spiders academic critics weave
such overwrought webs to maze
even the simplest tale, swaddling the fly
in so much tightly wound philosophy,
mere readers fail
to reconnect with the shock of what they saw –
the glistening dew drifted between two branches
that startled the day awake.

Tabloid

SEX BOMB TERROR GANG MYSTERY!
BOMB MYSTERY SEX GANG TERROR!
TERROR GANG MYSTERY SEX BOMB!
GANG TERROR BOMB MYSTERY SEX !
MYSTERY BOMB SEX TERROR GANG!

In three-piece suits

In three-piece suits and finely honed smiles, the diplomats
settle their border disputes.
Long before the stockyards come in sight
cattle herded in wagons smell their death.

The rules of war

Forget the Geneva Convention!
Who are we kidding? Courts
have no jurisdiction here. The only
rule of war is to win. Anything else
reeks of apology.

Incident in a revolution

While the professor, the party's leading spokesman,
was sifting reports of numbers killed and other data
of the day's progress, he was disturbed to find
some of his cohorts standing behind his armchair
with a large bundle.
They had brought home to him from the marketplace
a ragged clump of blood and bone mixed in with gravel.
"Your daughter" they told him. "Our plastic bombs
have not been taught yet to discriminate".

Survivor

As we stake out the road to the Delta container dock,
offer leaflets to truckers, telling them of
the Israeli shipping line, Zim,
whose cargoes they'll soon be unloading,
and what that state had done to the people of Gaza,
I glance at my wrist. In case we get arrested
the cellphone number of a civil rights lawyer
is inked on my arm.
But my protest is only skin deep, these digits
are not indelible.

Return

"In the refugee camp after the Naqba my mother and father
were both constantly knitting fishing nets.
When I asked them why they told me
'The day you return to Tiberias, our old village,
this way you'll have everything ready to start afresh.'
My parents, now buried in all but memory,
assured me the deeds to their house by the shore
are valid still and merely await my return."

Fireworks two miles away

across the Ottawa River assault
this warm August night. Whenever
their barrage starts up I wonder
what they are celebrating?
Or is this Sarajevo?

Commercial break

Do you suffer from nausea, irritability,
nervousness, paranoia? Do you wake at night
with your brain tips going numb? Does your vision blur
when you turn on the TV?
Relax. Your condition's quite normal. You are living
in the twenty first century. Sadly, no cure has been found
whose side effects are not fatal.
Better luck in your next life!

Night vision

God has night vision. As we crawl forwards,
dreaming of safety in what we think is our camouflage,
his searchlights pick us out and we are gone.

Late night final

Early this morning a War Office spokesman said
"Nearly two thirds of the world's population is dead.
The experiment went off as well as could be expected"
God, it appears,
has sent down observers.

Growth potential

Yesterday I sowed a seed of doubt. Tonight
I shelter under its branches.

Index of first lines / words

AUTHOR PROFILE

Christopher Levenson, who was born in London, England and came to Canada in 1968, taught English and Creative Writing for 31 years at Carleton University, Ottawa. He co-founded and was first editor of *Arc* poetry magazine, as well as serving as series editor for the five-year existence of the Harbinger Poetry Series, which published exclusively first books of poetry. He also founded and ran the Arc Reading series in downtown Ottawa and was for a year Poetry Editor of the *Literary Review of Canada*.

Since moving to Vancouver in 2007 he helped revive and run the Dead Poets Reading series. and founded a book club, SALinE specifically for South Asian literature in English.

Apart from poetry, he has been active as a reviewer and as a translator from Dutch and German, and is working on an autobiography and *My word!*, a book about the current state of the English language.

CPSIA information can be obtained
at www.ICGtesting.com
Printed in the USA
BVHW052307090622
639366BV00006B/81

9 781774 032152